How to Remember Absolutely Everything

written by Herbie
illustrated by Barbara Vagnozzi

This book will show you how to remember absolutely everything.

Instructions to do something will appear in boxes like this.

How to remember things

You can remember things the hard way or the easy way.

The hard way is to repeat what you are trying to remember over and over, like your nine times table.

The easy way is to make pictures in your head.

Try this Shut your eyes and make a picture of your home in your head. Imagine you are opening your front door. Imagine you are walking in. Imagine you are going from one room to another until you have visited every room.

That's not so hard, is it? It's just like day-dreaming.

And by making those day-dream pictures, you have already started to build yourself …
memory with muscles!

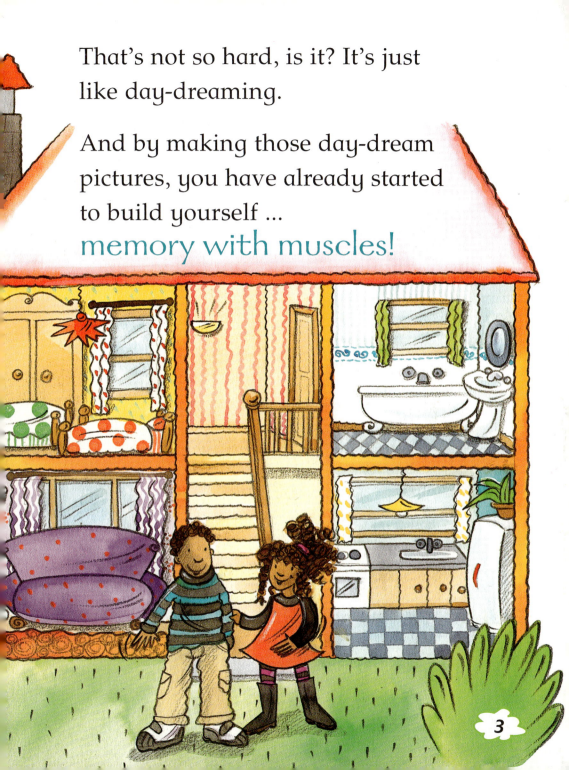

Read the list

Suppose you want to remember this list.

book	duck pond
apple	scissors
cat	knickers
tree	ice cream cone
television	hot-air balloon

Try this Read the list then turn the book over and see how many items you can remember. Then come back to the book and read on.

You probably remembered the knickers because they are funny. But how many more things did you remember? One? Two? Maybe three?

There are ten items on the list. If you make a picture of each one in your head, you will soon be able to remember every word in the right order. You will even be able to recite the list backwards.

The big secret to remembering the list is to make pictures in your head of each item *inside* your home.

Make pictures in your head

Here's how to do it.

Try this

- Make a picture of your home in your head just like you did before. See yourself outside the front door.

- Now see yourself leaving a book on the front doorstep. Make it a big book so everybody will trip over it trying to get in.

- Open the front door and put an apple in the hall. Make it a giant apple so you have to climb over it to get past.

Do you understand what you need to do? You are putting each item on the list inside your home, in the right order.

Put each item from the list in a different place in your home as you walk through it.

> **Try this**
>
> - Stick polka dots on the cat and put it down in one place. Make each item bigger than it would be in real life, and make it brighter and funnier too.
>
> - Put the tree in the sitting room and watch it sink its roots right through the best carpet.
>
> - The bigger and brighter and funnier your pictures are, the easier they will be to remember.

Try this

- Put the television halfway up the stairs and make it do a dance.

- Put the duck pond in a bedroom. Imagine the water seeping through the door and the ducks running everywhere!

- Imagine a giant pair of scissors made from ribbons.

You know what's coming next, don't you?

Try this   Make a picture of the knickers in your house!

Make them great big red frilly knickers with a smiley face across the bottom.

As you imagine each item on your list, make it bigger, make it brighter, make it silly, make it rude, make it funny. Do this any way you want to.

Try this Now imagine the ice cream cone. (Don't eat it.) Make it a really big ice cream cone, bigger than you are. Watch it start to melt all over … whatever you want.

Next imagine the hot-air balloon. Is it trying to lift off the roof? Does it nearly fill the bathroom?

Well done. Now you have gone through the whole list.

Don't try to remember the list. You don't need to. Just be sure to make each item big, bright, silly, funny or rude. All the items are inside your head, and no one can see them.

You can make your items move as well. The cat could do a tap-dance. The scissors might be playing football.

You can put more than one item in a room. Just leave each item in a different place.

> **Try this** Make each picture as clear as you can. Close your eyes and see it in your mind. (Once you get used to making pictures like this, you'll find you can do it with your eyes open.)

And now it is time to find out if this method works.

Don't try to remember

Close this book or cover up the list.
Don't try to remember.
Get out a pencil and a sheet of paper.
Don't try to remember.
Close your eyes.
Don't try to remember.

Try this

- Imagine you are standing at the front door of your home. What's that on the doorstep? A giant **book**, that's what. It's the first item on your list. Open your eyes and write it down.

- Now close your eyes again and walk through your home the way you did before.

- Each time you see an item on the list, open your eyes and write it down.

- Keep going until you've been in every room. Write down every item you see.

How did you do?

You might not have written down all ten items. But you will have remembered more items from the list than you did *without* making pictures in your head. It's almost impossible not to.

✓ book
✓ apple
✓ cat
tree
✓ television
duck pond
✓ scissors
✓ pair of knickers
✓ ice cream cone
✓ hot-air balloon

As you get used to making pictures in your head, you'll remember more and more. You will be able to remember the whole list in the right order, just by walking through your home the same way you did when you made the pictures.

You can even remember the list backwards by starting with the last room you walked into, and walking back to your front door.

But that's not all.

Remember even more

The list in this book was only ten items long. But it's just as easy to remember 20, 25 or even more items.

You won't remember every item first time, but you'll remember a lot. And as you get used to making pictures, you'll remember more and more.

Trip to the seaside.
Remember to bring:
- Swimming kit
- Money for rides

In the end, you will remember every item, every time.

You can use pictures in your head to help you remember other things as well as lists.

Try making pictures of the things your teacher tells you. They are so much easier to remember that way.

And if you are asked to do something, try this …

Suppose your mum or dad asks you to buy some bread from the corner shop on your way home from school tomorrow.

Try this Picture the outside of the corner shop. Now picture a giant loaf of bread poking out through the window.

That's all you have to do. Tomorrow when you see the shop, it will trigger a memory of the loaf of bread.

You can set special triggers like that to help you remember things. It could be the school bell, a television programme, or the face of somebody you'll meet. When you hear the bell, or watch the programme, or meet the person, you'll remember what it is you wanted to remember.

Pictures make remembering things easy every time.

Now try this!

See if you can use your amazing memory muscles to remember all the items in this suitcase.

Index

apple 4, 6

book 4, 6, 15
bread 20
butterfly 4, 8

cat 4, 8, 12

duck pond 4, 9

hot-air balloon 4, 11

ice cream cone 4, 11

knickers 4, 10

money for rides 18

scissors 4, 9, 12
swimming kit 18

television 4, 9, 22
tree 4, 8